The Path to Calvary

Reflections on the Stations of the Cross

With lino cuts
by Mark Cazalet

ST PAULS

Illustrations: Lino cuts by Mark Cazalet

ST PAULS Publishing
187 Battersea Bridge Road
London SW11 3AS, UK

ISBN 085439 597 0

Set by TuKan DTP, Fareham, UK
Produced in the EC
Printed by AGAM, Cuneo, Italy

ST PAULS is an activity of the priests and brothers
of the Society of St Paul who proclaim the Gospel
through the media of social communication

Foreword

The Stations of the Cross

From the earliest times Christians travelled to the Holy Land to visit the sites hallowed by Christ. Their devotions tended to focus on the sufferings of Jesus, attracting them to the places where he was thought to have halted on his way from the praetorium to Golgotha. Many ardently desired to make such a pilgrimage, but lacked the means. Possibly such yearning was somewhat assuaged after the fifth century, when the first known 'Stations (or Way) of the Cross', to be erected outside the Holy Land, was placed on the walls of the church of San Stefano in Bologna. In those days a varying number of scenes depicted an incident in the Passion of Christ, assisting and encouraging the faithful to 'accompany' the Lord in the final act of his suffering.

Making the Way of the Cross became increasingly widespread with the return of the crusaders in the twelfth and thirteenth centuries, some of whom erected tableaux to commemorate the holy places they had visited. This practice was adopted by many religious and most notably by the Franciscan friars to whom custody of the shrines of the Holy Land was given in 1342. From then on pictorial representations of the events of the Passion were placed on the walls and in the grounds of most religious houses. Meditating on these Stations became so popular that the erection of a 'Way of the Cross' quickly spread to parish churches. Finally in the eighteenth century the

Church regularised the custom by stipulating the fourteen incidents that were to be included in the devotion and the conditions under which indulgences could be received.

This custom of praying at the Stations in order to be united in Christ's Passion survived the radical changes of Vatican II, which swept away a number of ancient practices. Hence by the end of the century a 'Way of the Cross' was still to be found in most Catholic churches and chapels, and also in gardens, and in places of pilgrimage. It was a popular form of common and private prayer much used during the season of Lent.

A Personal Note

There were many reasons why I was attracted to this particular way of praying. Brought up as a Liberal Jew, at the age of twenty one I was instructed in the faith while I was at college. But being impatient by nature, I chafed at the twelve long months that I had to wait for baptism. During this time, I entered upon every pious custom from the lighting of candles to saying the rosary. Then I happened to find the prayers of the Way of the Cross set out in the drab looking *Simple Prayer Book*. At that stage I had no notion of how to set about praying and here were simple instructions, accompanied by the physical activity of kneeling, standing and walking from one Station to the next. I began to make the Stations on Fridays and on every day but Sunday during Lent.

At the same time I was reading avidly, for the most part with greater devotion than comprehension. Deeply moved by the Gospel of St John, I erroneously drew the conclusion that the main responsibility for the death of Jesus lay with the Jews. What better vehicle than the Stations, therefore, through which to pour out my sorrow and compassion? So this prayer had become integral to my faith life by the time that I learnt that all had some part in the crucifixion of Christ.

By that time I was no longer content to say the 'Our Father', 'Hail Mary' and 'Glory be,' as directed by my *Simple Prayer Book*, and was adding petitions and explaining their importance in long conversations with Jesus. My eyes were gradually opening to the suffering of the world; I felt privileged and powerless, but received some comfort from sharing the burden with Jesus.

My vocation to the Society of the Sacred Heart developed alongside my faith. It was therefore a bitter blow when an old spinal injury became a bar to the clean bill of health that was then required by Canon Law of every candidate to religious life. I did not understand that it was possible to ask for admission a second time, and the aching desire to become a religious of the Society never left me. It was a desire that entered all my prayer and especially that of 'the Stations of the Cross.' Thirteen years later a favourable medical finally achieved the longed for admission, but as I spent my noviceship convinced that I was within a whisper of being sent home – I never totally maintained the rule of silence – the Stations, often said on my bed at night, remained a staple prayer of serious petition.

Once, as a penance, for a misdemeanour now long

forgotten, I was told to 'make the Stations' but to stop short before reaching the Crucifixion. My novice mistress would not have known how this was to affect me. Without warning I became immersed in an experience of the inconsolable grief of being cut off from God. This was followed by a clearer understanding of the cost that Christ bore to fashion a bridge leading back to his Father. Such Pauline texts as "He emptied Himself", (Phil 2:7) assumed deeper, more poignant meaning. At that moment of grace, the fear of wrongdoing was transformed to a desire to love. Countless times since I have failed in love, but the grace of that experience remains with me still.

I have been, indeed I am, richly blessed by God, not least in prayer. May God grant that all who unite with Christ on His 'Path to Calvary' discover and radiate the love of His Heart. And if by the use of this small book, one person glorifies the Heart of Christ, making known the love of God, its purpose will have been achieved.

Frances Makower

Introduction

During his brief lifespan Jesus appeared to have vanquished darkness; lepers were cleansed, the deaf heard, the blind gained sight and the dead were raised... but then at the end his followers fled. He was crucified and broad noon turned pitch night.

'I will be with you all days' he had said, surely a promise beyond belief in these dark days, where evil flows unchecked, and his words ring hollow. Are we striving to keep faith with a braggart?

Yet in the tomb there were women who dared to confront his death and they found him. Have we their courage? Can we face the anguish of broken lives and find strength to seek out the sorrowing? Will he not, as in life, be there among them; and when we find him, will he not bring us back to his Father?

Jesus is condemned to death

Jesus is condemned to death

I watch you, Jesus, cold and hungry, consumed by demands of limitless love. You gave yourself to your disciples. They betrayed you. Now, deliberately passive, you stand before Pilate encompassed by unmitigated malice. Paradoxically, your very passivity breaks irrevocably the bondage of evil.

Looking around I see, alongside this Jerusalem drama, a great crowd of women, men and children as they pass before my inner eye. They, too, have been the toys of tyrants, were shamelessly broken – unjustly discarded. Forgetful for once, of self, I grieve for these people, grieve for each individual son and daughter made in the loving image of God.

But by what right do I, a cowardly bystander, stand and stare as my dry tongue tangles with useless words? I can no more hide from the imaged atrocities as they unroll in my head than I can deny that, busied with the affairs of self, I have both heard and ignored those broken cries. In truth I have become entrapped in personal ease; I am absorbed by my rights, my comfort, my ever-increasing slice of the cake. Frozen footed and frozen hearted, sickened by the certainty that my selfishness has played its part in the power of evil, I stand shamed and helpless.

Jesus receives the cross

Jesus receives the cross

B undled hither and there, you neither speak nor waver. Not a word as you submit to bullying guards; silent as they parade you before the depraved and pampered Herod; wordlessly you receive the cross. And thus as you drink your bitter cup, you transform this cross of death into a symbol of living hope.

Repelled and yet compelled, once more I watch with inward eye. I see a motley crowd from every age and every nation. People who have been despised, beaten or tortured simply because they could not conform. Some owned no worse than a pallid skin, or a face that was framed by dark, tight curls; others had looked on the world through almond eyes; for others the offence lay in a garment – a saffron robe, a veil or a turban; even David's star stitched to a tattered coat was accounted criminal. Some were judged too old or too young, others too sick or too useless.

I am confused. What brings these broken people to Calvary? Why do they batten on my concern? Gradually, shamefully, comprehension dawns. These, like Christ, are innocent victims. They suffered because they differed in faith or custom and have refused to surrender integrity. As for me, have I not contributed to the crippling climate of prejudice? At best I have raised neither voice nor hand in protest; at worst I have actively oppressed. Dear Lord, you died for all. Forgive us. Forgive me. Help us to love. Help me to love by deed, no less than by word.

Jesus falls for the first time

Jesus falls for the first time

You stagger forward, Lord, one step then two; your persistent YES culminating in Calvary's summit. Your obedience is total, but the path is steep, the load crushing and the guards irascible. You fall and they, exasperated, curse and kick. I see your broken body struggle, for your hour is indeed upon you.

Hesitant, but by now expectant, I search for those around you. Few are famous, the majority unknown. Some died of the diseases they had come to cure, others risked their lives because they cared. Many who worked among the poor have been 'disposed of'; wealthy tyrants are so often paranoid.

With small desire to remain, I am strangely reluctant to move; the knowledge that in my time I have also oppressed, impedes me. For I have read the papers and watched TV and may not plead ignorance. Now and then I have dared to raise objections, but quietly; it is risky work to attract attention, and disapproval is uncomfortable. My personal affairs leave little time for the less fortunate. A great gulf yawns between my ease and your selfless love. At last I prepare to leave and, turning, catch sight of your bridge, the bridge that you gave your life to build. Oh that I could at least desire to desire to approach that bridge. Dare I ask for the strength to enable me to put one foot in front of the other, as I slowly, so slowly, make my way back to the Father.

Jesus meets his mother

Jesus meets his mother

Mary, you wait; sinister rumours circle. Faith is stretched to breaking point, until at long, long last, the ugly procession winds into view. 'This is the man. There goes Jesus of Nazareth,' they say. Can this be? Is this broken body, with back bowed and face streaming blood, your son? Jesus, sensing your presence, raises his head; your eyes meet. Strength, engendered by love, flows from the encounter.

Shoulder to shoulder, a group of women stand tall, alongside Mary. Irrationally clinging to hope, they have succoured sons and daughters in drought and famine. They have nursed fevered children, cradled their own and their neighbours' sick and ceaselessly risked their lives. With stubborn strength endowed by careless love they would not give up, but continued to demand, 'Where are the disappeared?'

Where you go, Mary, Jesus will follow. Was it not your YES made at the cost of such personal havoc, that formed the framework for Jesus' bridge back to the Father? Mary, midwife and mother, when we, when I abandon your son, guide me back to that bridge. Say to me, as you said to the servants at Cana, 'Do whatever he tells you.'

Simon of Cyrene carries the cross

Simon of Cyrene carries the cross

Jesus' strength is failing. The soldiers panic; afraid of the frenzied crowd, lusting after their sport. The Captain orders a halt; meantime, Simon of Cyrene, a stranger in Jerusalem, senses danger. He lunges against the flow of the mob, determined as ever to break free from trouble. But his height and obvious strength attract attention. 'Seize that man,' the Captain yells. 'Give him the cross!' Simon finds himself manhandled into the centre of the very drama from which he was escaping. Enraged and bewildered, he trips. The transverse beam crashes onto the victim – but for the quick-witted sergeant both would have fallen. Petrified, Simon is brought face to face with Jesus; anger and panic ebb as Simon welcomes rare peace.

There are many Simons on Calvary. Some have eagerly risked comfort or even life for friend, stranger or foe; more, like Simon of Cyrene, have said an immediate NO, only to back-track and discover eleventh-hour courage. All are everyday beings who remind us that given grace, the weakest may find strength to stand beside the powerless.

I, too, have turned my back on trouble. I mean to play the 'Good Samaritan', but when the need is upon me I cannot break free from personal concerns. Lord, in your mercy, re-set my inner compass. Direct me to my neighbours' need. Give me both desire and strength to transform my NO into your constant YES.

Veronica wipes the face of Jesus

Veronica wipes the face of Jesus

The situation seems hopeless! Simon offers physical strength but no one can pierce the pall of evil, until a flash of movement takes an unknown woman past the cordon of guards. With infinite compassion, Veronica – as her action has named her – wipes the face of Jesus, and for a timeless moment, before her arrest, love outwits brute force. What reckless folly! She could staunch neither blood nor pain, why risk so much for so little?

Yet Veronica, no less than Simon, has companions. Beside her stand parents who risked death to remain beside doomed children, aid workers who relentlessly rebuilt the ever breaking bridges, peacemakers who destroyed themselves as they absorbed the poisons of hatred; all fools in the eyes of the world, but these are the unsung heroes who have believed, loved and hoped beyond reasonable expectation.

Constantly to unravel the re-tied knot and to forswear bitterness, opposition and apathy, costs dear. In human terms the results will never balance. But if we, if I, fail in such relentless love, how can I be his follower? I pray that like Veronica my love will outrun reason.

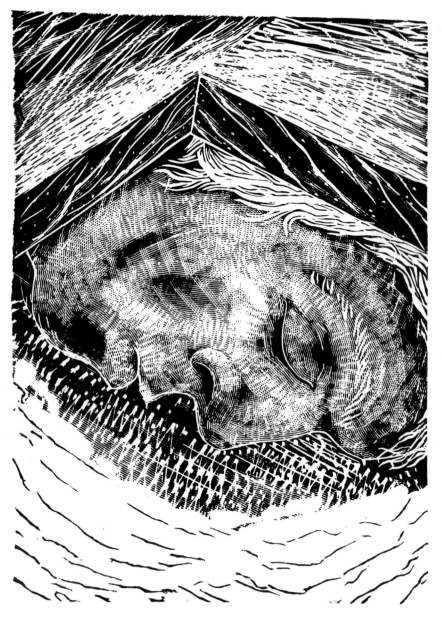

Jesus falls a second time

Jesus falls a second time

Mary, Simon, Veronica, each has been swept aside as this cosmic climax mounts. Love empowers, but cannot annihilate destructive evil. And so you fall again. Your broken body is jarred afresh; wounds re-opened. The frantic soldiers drag, lash and bludgeon you onto your feet. Staggering, you shuffle forward and the crowd cheers as the spectacle resumes.

Alone, yet not alone! Around you gather every woman, man and child as, girded or tortured beyond endurance, they lose their lives.

As for me, I am shamed by the speed of my complaints. I sulk over a petty, personal slight. My world shrinks as an irrational grudge inflates to an intolerable burden. Painfully, I acknowledge the true proportions of my privileged position. Forgive me, forgive us all our all-consuming centredness of self. Hold us steadfast as together we stumble along the Way.

The women weep for Jesus

The women weep for Jesus

The pathetic procession drags along with few to respond to the prisoner's plight. Only a handful of women – friends and colleagues – stand apart, silently mourning. Their tears flowed as they watched Veronica's passionate, pointless, defiance; and when Jesus falls a second time they weep without restraint. Jesus is crushed; he is absorbed in personal pain and yet he can find the strength to reach out to his companions. 'Dry your tears,' he tells them. 'The future will claim your sorrow.'

Gradually the group of women are joined by insignificant ones and twos who have come to take their place on Calvary. Their presence proclaims that neither fear nor brutality can crush compassion.

I am drawn to these women; they challenge me. I watch in awe the young and old, women and men who have earned their place on Calvary. I yearn to join them. Each has learnt and offered the cost of love. Is it possible that I, too, might learn?

Jesus falls a third time

Jesus falls a third time

The two thieves have already reached 'the Place of the Skull', but Jesus has fallen behind. Simon is tiring; he loses his foothold, the cross slips from his grasp and Jesus is felled yet again. While soldiers struggle with entangled limbs, the bloodthirsty mob surrounds them. The scene is set for a lynching. 'Stand back', roars the Captain, as he returns and resumes control. One guard yanks Jesus to his feet, another heaves the cross from the ground until finally, cursing, sweating and shoving, they haul Jesus up to Calvary's summit.

Calvary is awash with humanity. All whose lives have been broken, destroyed or stunted are assembled there.

One glance is enough for me. I have neither voice nor tears and my legs are leaden. I am held captive by the knowledge that my callous indifference, selfish demands and lust for power have added, in part at least, to the tragedy of all these lives. 'Forgive me,' I whisper, 'for the sake of your Jesus, forgive me...'

Jesus is stripped of his clothes

Jesus is stripped of his clothes

Betrayed and deserted, pushed to the edge of endurance, on Golgotha Jesus loses the last fragment of human dignity as his clothes are ripped from his body. He is naked, vulnerable, despised. The powers of darkness have their way, yet he remains the victor: a mystery which can be neither denied nor explained. His life has rebuilt an eternal bridge to carry all who are willing back to the Father.

An eerie stillness covers the hill; I am expectant, looking around me for the companions of Jesus. With increasing unease, I extend my gaze to the wider landscape. My eyes focus on waterlogged craters in which bloated, lifeless creatures float; broad, gaping gashes criss-cross through uprooted forests where slashed timber lies on barren earth. In the mid-distance choking dust belches from tall chimneys while stunted, apathetic beings toil below. The earth seems to have been as effectively stripped as the body of Jesus.

Living with green and plenty I would like to forget those lifeless lands, but I cannot. I know both too little and too much. The greenhouse effect, desertification, the unjust, unequal provision of water, food and fuel are both obvious and deceptively simple. I may not know how to redress these problems, but I understand that greed plays a major part and in greed, I'm an expert. Oh Jesus, as you lie stripped and forsaken, I beg the grace of simplicity. Help me to desire less, that others may have more.

Jesus is nailed to the cross

Jesus is nailed to the cross

'He's almost gone, don't waste the cup!' one said, as the executioner prepared hammer and nails. They were seasoned men but could not stomach the screams and gave spiced wine to the victims to dull their senses. 'Let be', said the other, but Jesus pushed the drink away. His ultimate YES must be fulfilled in total consciousness. The crowd was hushed, some even covered their ears, and as the last nail was finally driven home, many were openly weeping. Then when the three crosses were hoisted aloft, releasing the people from the oppressive proximity of pain, they returned to their carefree roistering.

The group that surrounds the hill top is unexpected; there is not a leader among them. They are the ones who have carried the can, lit the torches, pressed the triggers or loosed the bombs, while at a safe distance the Pilates busily washed their hands.

How can this be? Lord, did you fail, meekly surrendering to evil? Where was your Father? How could true love allow defeat? And if you cannot save yourself, what hope for us, what hope for the future? Where's the point of a world in which truth and good faith are annihilated by those very beings whom God has created and continues to hold in being? As these questions rattle around in my head, I am aware that answers, in part at least, must rest with my own response. In some mysterious way, I know that only by going on, going on, will I receive some glimmer of meaning. My God, I am frightened!

Jesus dies on the cross

Jesus dies on the cross

The nails have torn his flesh, his life blood ebbs. The crowds jostle, gape and jeer, the authorities gloat and the soldiers dice indifferently; fear hangs thick in the pitch dark, black.

'Forgive them, they know not what they do', pardon secured for every crime of every age.

'This day you will be with me in paradise' – promise bestowing universal hope.

The third hour drags into completion. The Temple curtain rips. 'My God, my God, why have you forsaken me?'

Thus in an insignificant colony one individual suffered all evil; he absorbed within himself the total sum of suffering for every woman, man or child. He suffered to rebuild in his own humanity the bridge leading freely in and out of love's territory. His loving became the most potent powerlessness the world will witness.

I watch in full knowledge that I am no innocent bystander. Have I not betrayed employer, friend or child; lied, stolen or cheated to serve twisted needs? By symbol, if not in act, I have swung both hammer and scourge. My God, have mercy. At the foot of the cross I dare to plead, in the very name of your suffering son. Father, forgive; forgive us all.

Jesus is taken down from the cross

Jesus is taken down from the cross

The heart had gone from the drama. Jesus is palpably dead and the crowd is drifting away. The priests have already left. To avoid defilement they must dispose of the body before sundown brings in the Passover Feast; to their chagrin, for this they must seek the permission of Pilate. For his friends, alone at last, there is freedom to vent their grief. They gather around Mary, his mother, while John, to whose care she is left, vainly tries to make her leave. The sudden rhythm of marching feet, heard by them all, causes panic. Pilate, giving in to the priests, had ordered a posse of guards to return to Calvary. 'Don't touch him', the women scream, 'he's dead!' In disbelief one of the soldiers pierces his side with a lance and immediately blood and water flows out. 'Help us', the women beg. One of the guards responds and lifts him down from the cross, giving the corpse to his mother; with reluctance Mary surrenders her son.

So Mary joined the countless mothers helplessly watching the death of their own. Among them were many denied even the raw comfort of funeral rites: few had a grave they could tend, for most of the loved ones of these women were among those officially unknown, conveniently 'disappeared'.

I am both afraid and confused; the separation of death is violent, inescapable, final. I had heard his words and I had thought I believed, but now the dream is betrayed, all hope proved hollow and life seems utterly worthless.

Jesus is buried

Jesus is buried

Pilate was in a murderous mood. Their man was dead and now they were quarrelling over his corpse; first the priests, and then Nicodemus and Joseph of Arimathea, both too wealthy to be ignored. Let them fight it out without him, had not Pilate washed his hands of the whole affair? But Joseph and Nicodemus paid scant attention to Romans; their urgent task was to get the corpse into some decent grave before the onset of the festival froze all activity. There was no time for the niceties of ritual observance. Later the women could attend to that. They had at least secured a grave in a private garden. Dusk was already falling as they finally heaved a great boulder in front of the entrance. His death, no less than his birth, was hurried, makeshift and beyond the control of friends or kinsfolk.

Those generous and courageous men are not alone. Many have shared possessions, risked ridicule, freedom and even life to help friend or stranger in desperate straits. In famine, war or flight there have always been selfless Samaritans prepared, at personal cost, to assist the oppressed.

I seem to have been watching the work of sin in which I have undoubtedly played my part. I am terror-struck by the vicious, destructive force unleashed, but I have also witnessed the power of love. At this moment I am alone and frightened, dangling between fear and hope. I cannot forget all that has been said and done; these mixed memories contain a frail promise for our world. Lord, help me, help us all to keep faith through darkening days.

Jesus rises from the dead

Jesus rises from the dead

It was very early on the first day of the week and still dark, when Mary of Magdala came to the tomb. She saw that the stone had been moved away and came running to Peter. 'They have taken the Lord out of the tomb,' she said, 'and we don't know where they have put him.' So Peter set out... Mary stood outside the tomb, weeping. She turns and sees Jesus standing there, but she does not know him.

'Woman, why are you weeping?'
'They have taken my Lord away', she replied.
'Mary!'
'Rabbuni!'

Time and again, Jesus comes to each of us and we fail to see him as our lives weave fitfully between small deaths and resurrection. The gift of Jesus' life brought us the Trinity: mysterious community of love and model of human relating. As we are imaged in Jesus, the Son of the Father, may his Spirit enable us to recognise Jesus in every neighbour and may we, in turn, be recognised for disciples as we strive to live in love.

Questions for reflection or discussion, alone or in groups

1. Why do you think the Stations have remained a continuously popular form of prayer?

2. Have you ever thought of writing your own 'Stations'? Would you want to add or omit some incidents? Why?

3. Which Station appeals to you most strongly? Can you explain why?

4. Can you suggest different ways of praying the Stations?

5. What do you think prompted Simon and Veronica to act as they did?

6. Whom do you think are the Simons and Veronicas of today? Do you know anyone who fulfils their roles?

7. What do you think is meant by "filling up" the sufferings of Christ?

8. How can we strengthen those who are suffering today?

9. Jesus is described as speaking with authority. How do you think this manifested itself? Do you know, or know of, others who also speak with authority? What marks them out?

10. Do you have problems forgiving? Have you been able to share your feelings with anyone? Can you pray for the grace that would enable you to forgive?

11. Lent is sometimes thought of as a time of denial. Do you adopt Lenten practices? What do you think is the real point of giving something up for Lent?

12. What do you think is the basis of prejudice? What feeds and what dispels prejudice?

13. Could you share something of your own 'path to Calvary'? If you are on your own, write it down. Have you surprised yourself?

14. In recent years it has been customary to add the Resurrection as a fifteenth Station, but many people oppose the practice. What would you do and why?

15. Did Mary, the mother of Christ, have any warning of what would happen to her Son? How and from whom could she hope for comfort?